ERRATA

A BOOK OF HISTORICAL ERRORS

Illustrated by HEMESH ALLES

Written by A.J. WOOD
Historical consultant WILLIAM CROUCH

STEWART
HOUSE

To my mother for all her encouragement — H.A.

Published in Canada in 1992 by Stewart House,
481 University Avenue, Toronto, Ontario M5G 2E9.

Devised and produced by The Templar Company plc,
Pippbrook Mill, London Road, Dorking, Surrey RH4 1JE, Great Britain.

Designed by Mike Jolley
Manufactured in Italy

Canadian Cataloguing-in-Publication Data

Alles, Hemesh
Errata

ISBN 1-895246-26-1

1. Civilization, Ancient — Juvenile literature.
2. Picture puzzles — Juvenile literature.
I. Wood, A.J., 1960-   II. Title.
CB311.A55   1992   j930   C92-093661-X

Introduction

TURN THE pages of this book and you will find twelve scenes from history.

See what life was like in ancient Egypt 4,000 years ago. Visit an Aztec

city on market day. Discover how Christmas was celebrated in Norman England.

Join an aboriginal kangaroo hunt.

Look carefully at each of the twelve pictures. Can you spot ten things in

each one that are wrong? You may find an Inca warrior reading a newspaper,

a streetlight illuminating a Viking feast, or a zebra hiding among a group

of horses in a Sioux Indian encampment.

If you get stuck, just turn to the back of the book and all the

answers will be revealed, along with some fascinating information about

what life was like in the past.

*F*arming on the banks of the Nile in ancient Egypt

OVER 4,000 years ago, the ancient Egyptians formed a great kingdom in northern Africa. It was one of the world's earliest, and at its heart was a great river — the Nile.

The Egyptians were great farmers, architects, and scholars. The carvings on their great stone temples and pyramids provide us with a picture of what life was like in Egypt many thousands of years ago.

Aboriginal kangaroo hunt in Australia's Northern Territory

AUSTRALIA'S FIRST inhabitants came to the continent from Southeast Asia about 40,000 years ago. They were nomadic people who traveled throughout the country hunting and gathering food. They treated their land and its creatures with great respect, and made them the basis of their religion and sacred law.

When European settlers arrived in Australia in the late 18th century, they called the natives "aboriginals," meaning people who had lived there since the earliest times.

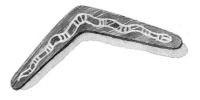

*T*he arrival of the bridal party at a Zulu wedding

IN ABOUT 1000 A.D., the ancestors of the Zulu traveled south from central Africa, settling the hilly grassland that they still occupy today.

In the early 19th century the Zulus developed as a separate tribe. They lived in homesteads called *kraals,* each one housing a headman and his relatives. Marriage involved an arrangement between two homesteads, and the traditional Zulu wedding was surrounded by ceremonial events of great importance.

4

*P*owwow at a Sioux Indian encampment

WITH THE Great Plains stretching behind them, a group of Sioux elders gather around a fire to smoke their pipe of peace.

The Sioux were noted for their bravery and fought many battles against the settlers who tried to take over their territory in the last half of the 19th century. At the Battle of Little Bighorn in 1876, they defeated the U.S. cavalry but were eventually driven, along with the other Indian tribes, onto reservations.

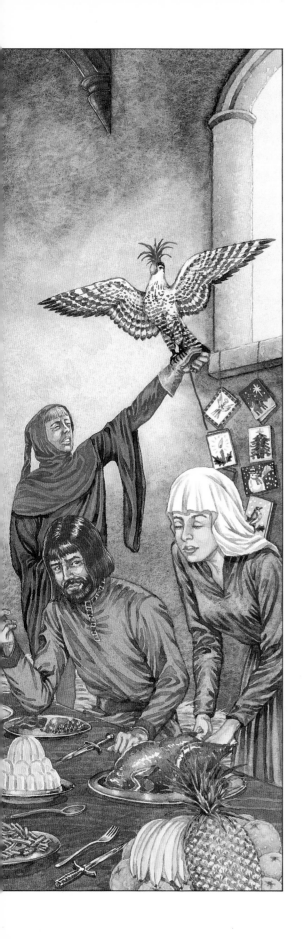

5

A feast to celebrate Christmas Day at the manor house of a Norman lord

IN 1066, French Normans invaded England and defeated the Saxons in the great Battle of Hastings. William the Conqueror became King of England and his appointed lords controlled their own land and servants from great estates, called manors.

Every manor had its manor house, and every house its great hall, and it was here that everyone gathered for a feast to celebrate Christmas Day.

*M*en return from a seal hunt to an Inuit encampment

MANY THOUSANDS of years ago, the Inuit people, originally from Asia, settled in the frozen Arctic — one of the last areas in the world to be colonized.

Once known as Eskimos, the Inuit, whose name means simply "people," were nomadic, hunting animals such as the seal, walrus, whale, and caribou to provide food and skins.

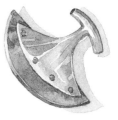

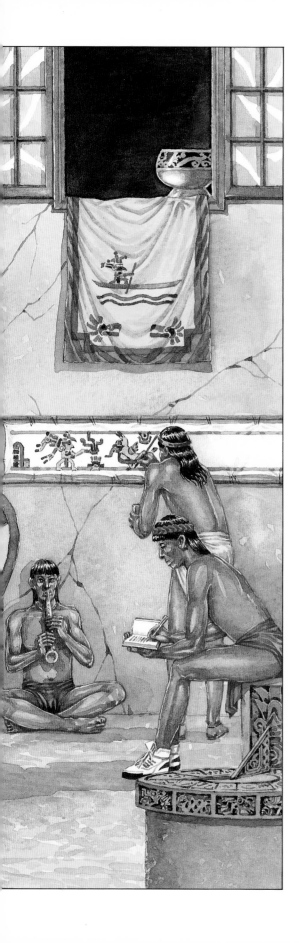

7

*F*estival day
in the great square of
Tenochtitlan, the Aztec's
city in the lake

THE AZTECS arrived on the shores of Lake
Texcoco in the Valley of Mexico in 1345. They
built their city on a tiny island in the lake and
soon became rich and powerful.

The Aztecs were fierce warriors,
imaginative artists, and hardworking farmers.
In the great square, markets were held and
festivals of the gods were celebrated with
singing, dancing, and sacrifices.

*T*he funeral of a Viking chief at Hedeby on the shores of the Baltic Sea

THE YEARS from the 8th to the 11th centuries marked the Age of the Vikings — fierce warriors who sailed south from their Scandinavian homelands to both terrorize and trade with peoples from Iceland to Africa, Asia to America.

The death of a chief was cause for great ceremony, the body being sent out to sea on a burning longboat to start its journey to Valhalla, the Viking heaven.

Celebration in the Mogul Court of Akbar

DURING THE 16th century, Akbar, the most important of India's Mogul emperors, came to power. He counted the great warrior Genghis Khan among his ancestors. During his reign, the Mogul empire spread to include almost all of present-day India.

Although Akbar could neither read nor write, he made his court a center of culture, encouraging the work of poets, artists, architects, and musicians.

Ships arriving in a Minoan port

FROM 3,000 B.C., the great Minoan civilization flourished for nearly 2,000 years on the island of Crete, near mainland Greece.

The Minoans built great palaces, decorated with beautiful paintings called frescoes. They sailed the Mediterranean Sea in fine wooden galleys, trading with the ancient Egyptians and Syrians. However, in 1450 B.C., a series of natural disasters (an earthquake, tidal wave, and volcanic eruption) brought their civilization to an end.

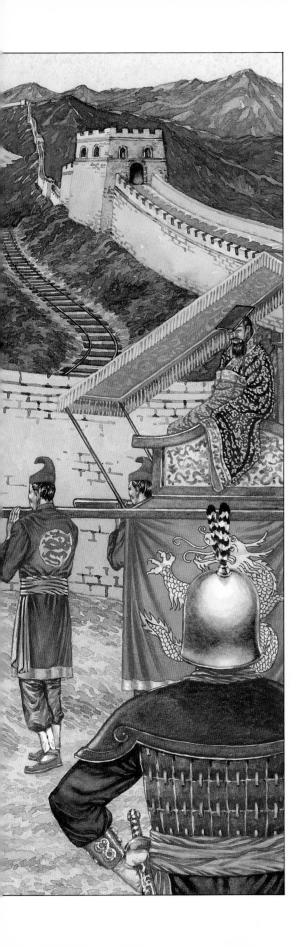

*T*he Emperor visits craftsmen near the Great Wall of ancient China

FOR MANY thousands of years, China's great empire was ruled by emperors who came from different dynasties or royal families.

During the Han dynasty, from 206 B.C. to 220 A.D., learning and art were greatly encouraged. Beautiful objects were fashioned from gold, silver, and jade. The Chinese were responsible for many inventions, such as paper, and ancient China enjoyed a time of peace and prosperity.

*T*he Inca army returns to the valley of Cuzco, high in the Peruvian Andes

BY THE end of the 15th century, a tribe of native American Indians, the Incas, controlled a huge empire that stretched more than 2,000 miles along the Pacific coast of South America.

From the capital city of Cuzco, the chief Inca controlled a powerful army and was worshipped as a god. But this great and wealthy empire was defeated in one short year. By 1533, the entire civilization had been destroyed by the conquering Spaniards.

Farming on the banks of the River Nile

1. The Egyptians, although great architects, did not build tower blocks or temples with domed roofs. Their greatest buildings were the pyramids — great burial chambers made of huge blocks of stone (**A**).

2. Ancient Egypt was ruled by a king, or pharaoh. He wore an elaborate headdress (**B**) rather than a crown, often decorated with symbols depicting the Egyptian gods.

3. The Egyptians did not use an alphabet of letters like ours. Instead, they used a form of picture writing known as hieroglyphics (**C**). One picture might represent one or two letters, or even a whole word.

4. The ancient Egyptians did not have books. They recorded information on papyrus scrolls (**D**) made from the pulped stems of the papyrus rush.

5. Farmers could not water their crops using a hose. Instead, they built a system of canals to help irrigate the dry land and used a shaduf (**E**) to raise the waters of the Nile from one level to another.

6. It would be unlikely to find an oak tree growing on the banks of the Nile. In Egypt's hot, dry climate, trees such as the date palm (**F**) would have been common. The Egyptians also grew figs and used trained baboons to pick them!

7. There were no tractors in ancient Egypt. The farmers used simple wooden plows pulled by oxen (**G**) to prepare the land for sowing. The seeds were scattered by hand and eventually harvested using flint-bladed sickles.

8. The fish that lived in the rich waters of the Nile were a valuable source of food. They would have been caught using a net or simple line and hook (**H**) rather than a fishing rod.

9. Crops were measured using ropes (**I**) rather than tape measures. This determined how much tax a farmer had to pay to the pharaoh.

10. The ancient Egyptians would not have had thermos flasks. They made pottery containers (**J**) to carry water, wine, and beer.

Aboriginal kangaroo hunt

1. You would not find a monkey swinging through the trees of the outback. Much of Australia's wildlife is unique and includes many animals that are found nowhere else in the world. Two examples are the koala (**A**) and the kangaroo.

2. There were no deer to hunt in Australia. Instead, the men hunted for fish, lizards, and kangaroos (**B**).

3. This aboriginal artist would not have known of elephants. His paintings were full of images of the animal and human ancestors (**C**) that aboriginals believe created the world before time began. They call this period of creation Dreamtime.

4. Paintings would not have been made using tubes of oil paint. Artists painted with sticks on flattened eucalpytus bark. Their paints were made from grinding natural ingredients such as clay, charcoal, and red and yellow ochre (**D**).

5. Hunters did not have jeeps or other vehicles to transport them across the bush. They traveled everywhere on foot (**E**).

6. You would not have found a dog, such as this red setter, accompanying the men through the outback. Instead, aboriginals used dingoes (**F**) and trained these wild dogs to help them during the hunt.

7. Aboriginals did not have bugles or any other musical instruments made of metal. They used a hollow branch called a didgeridoo (**G**) and wooden clapsticks to accompany their songs.

8. There were no crossbows to help aboriginals catch their prey. Instead they used nulla-nullas (hardwood clubs), woomeras (throwing sticks), and boomerangs (**H**).

9. You would not have found an African ostrich in the outback. However, similar looking birds called emus (**I**) are common there.

10. This aboriginal boy would not have sported a mermaid tattoo, but body paintings were an important part of aboriginal culture. These boys (**J**) are being painted as part of a series of rites that mark their entry into manhood.

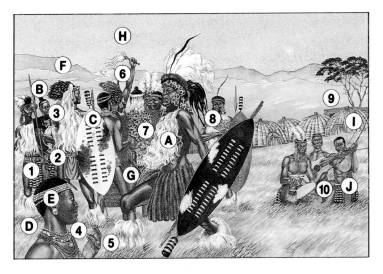

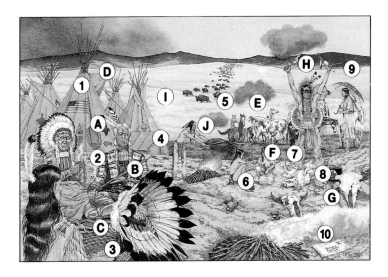

Zulu
wedding party

1. A Zulu warrior would not have worn a belt. His costume (**A**) would have been made of monkey or other animal hide, feathers, and cow's tails.

2. Zulus did not have swords. Instead, warriors used stabbing or throwing spears, and knobkerries, a kind of heavy wooden club (**B**).

3. The shields used by Zulus were not like this metal medieval shield. Theirs would have been made of ox-hide and measured the same height as a man (**C**).

4. A Zulu woman would not have worn a heart-shaped gold locket. Her jewelry would have consisted of carved wood or bone and, from the 1800s onwards, elaborate beadwork (**D**). The beads were increasingly obtained from European traders.

5. Although Africa is famous for its diamonds, this Zulu woman would not have had a diamond ring. The only "rings" she would have owned were ear-rings, worn as flat discs inside her ear lobes (**E**). Ear piercing took place for both girls and boys at the age of seven.

6. This headdress would not have contained peacock feathers since these birds were not known in Africa. Instead, it would have been decorated with ostrich feathers (**F**).

7. The bride would not have carried a bouquet of flowers as a Western bride might do. Instead, she carried a knife (**G**) as a symbol of her chastity. Her face was hidden by a veil of leaves — a mark of respect for the members of her new kraal.

8. The Zulus did not have fans like this paper one from China. They used fly whisks made of animal hair (**H**) to keep away insects.

9. The kraal would not have contained buildings made of brick. All the huts would have been beehive-shaped and made of saplings covered with grass thatch (**I**). The floor was made of clay and dung, polished so it shone like marble.

10. Rather than guitars, any music accompanying the wedding would have been played on traditional instruments such as drums, or ugubus (**J**) which are played like violins.

Sioux Indian
powwow

1. These native Americans would not have known this "Stars and Stripes," the U.S. national flag, since it only reached its present design in 1959. Their teepees would have been decorated with traditional symbols and designs (**A**).

2. The Sioux elders would have smoked a peace pipe (**B**) around the fire — which is very different in shape from a western-style pipe.

3. The elders of the tribe would not have sat on Tartan rugs made of wool. Their rugs, like much of their clothing, were woven from cotton with traditional motifs and designs (**C**).

4. The Sioux would not have had canvas tents. They lived in teepees made of buffalo hides stretched over a wooden frame. They lit fires inside the teepees (**D**) for cooking and warmth, and allowed the smoke to escape through flaps at the top.

5. Native Americans would not have known of the existence of African zebras. Wild mustangs (**E**) were highly prized and came in many colorings, from piebald to speckled.

6. Indian children would have played with simple toys carved from wood (**F**). They would not have known of teddy bears, invented in 1902 and named after President Theodore "Teddy" Roosevelt.

7. The medicine man would not have used a rhino's skull as part of his ritual. He would have used the skulls of cows or buffalo instead (**G**).

8. The medicine man, or shaman, would not have owned a first-aid kit. He practiced a different kind of medicine — offering sacrifices and praying to the spirit world for both the health and success of his tribe (**H**). He would have used natural materials and spells to heal illness.

9. This Indian squaw would not have owned an umbrella. Her teepee offered the only man-made shelter from the rain (**I**).

10. Native American tribes did not communicate using the postal system, which was introduced in the USA in 1753. Instead, they could send messages to neighboring tribes using smoke signals (**J**).

Norman feast on Christmas Day

1. You would not have found a Christmas tree in the great hall. Christmas trees were introduced into England from Germany in the early 1800s. Evergreen plants such as holly and ivy (**A**) would have been used for decoration.

2. Instead of a television, the Normans had to rely on the court jester (**B**) for entertainment.

3. A Norman knight might have had a hawk, not an owl, sitting on his wrist. Trained hawks (**C**) were used to hunt other birds such as pigeons and even swans.

4. The Normans did not have playing cards. After the feast, they played games such as Hoodman's Blind (**D**) which is similar to Blindman's Bluff.

5. There were no rugs on the manor floors. Instead, they were strewn with straw and rushes (**E**).

6. Great tapestries often hung from the walls of Norman houses. The most famous is the Bayeux Tapestry — which tells the story of the Battle of Hastings. In it you can see many examples of Norman transport (**F**). However, Normans did not ride bicycles. These would not be invented for hundreds of years.

7. No one would have been eating potato chips at a Norman banquet. The potato did not become popular in England until Sir Walter Raleigh brought it back from America in the 1590s. The meal would have included various fish and meats (**G**) and even peacock if the king was visiting! Poor people lived on vegetables such as peas and beans.

8. The Normans did not use forks. They ate with knives and spoons (**H**) but mostly used their fingers.

9. Tropical fruits such as pineapples and bananas were not known in Norman times. They grew apples (**I**) and grapes, and also made elaborate desserts sweetened with honey.

10. The custom of giving Christmas cards or presents was not known in Norman times. Christmas was one of several holidays, along with May Day and Midsummer Eve, all celebrated with feasting, singing, and dancing.

Inuit encampment

1. The Inuit did not live in wooden huts. During the freezing winter, they built shelters from blocks of snow, called igloos (**A**). At other times they made snow-covered tents of animal skins, or dug shelters into the ground with whalebone or driftwood roofs covered in turf.

2. The Inuit did not wash their clothes. In the sub-zero temperatures wet clothing would freeze solid in seconds! The only things likely to be hung on a line were animal skins (**B**) which would eventually be used to make clothing and bedding.

3. Snowmobiles were not invented until the 20th century. The traditional means of Inuit transport was a sled (**C**) made of whalebone covered with skins, or driftwood. Hunters used these to travel many miles in search of food.

4. The Inuit did not have running water. They melted ice in big cauldrons to provide water for cooking and cleaning (**D**).

5. This Inuit woman would not have worn a skirt made from zebra skin.

Most clothes were made from layers of caribou or polar bear skin (**E**).

6. Inuit do not have blond hair and fair skin. These people share the darker skin and straight black hair of their Asian ancestors (**F**).

7. Inuit could not grow vegetables in such a cold climate. For much of the year, they lived on a diet of fish and seal meat (**G**) eaten both cooked and raw. The word "eskimo" means "eater of raw meat".

8. The Inuit sleds were pulled by dogs called huskies (**H**). Horses would not have survived such harsh conditions.

9. Penguins have never inhabited the Arctic. They live at the opposite end of the earth — many thousands of miles away in the frozen Antarctic. The Arctic is home to many other birds, including the snowy owl (**I**).

10. This woolly mammoth became extinct about 10,000 years ago, long before Inuit arrived in the frozen north. The largest animal now living in the Arctic is the polar bear (**J**).

Festival day in Tenochtitlan

1. The Aztecs did not travel by airplane, which was not invented until 1903. Local journeys were undertaken in small flat-bottomed boats (**A**).

2. Although the Aztec's empire stretched from the shores of the Pacific to the Gulf of Mexico, it is unlikely that they would have known about giraffes which come from Africa. They would certainly have known about monkeys and jaguars (**B**) and animal motifs such as these were a familiar part of the decoration on clothes and carvings.

3. The Aztecs did not have wristwatches. They probably used sundials to tell the time (**C**).

4. There were no wheeled vehicles in Tenochtitlan because the city was criss-crossed with canals. Babies were not pushed in carriages, but were wrapped in cloth and carried on their mothers' backs (**D**).

5. Walkmans were not known to the Aztecs, but they were very musical people. They played pipes (**E**) and drums.

6. The Aztecs did not play basketball as it is played today. They did play a game called tlachtli. The ball for this game (**F**) was made of rubber, and the players hit it with their elbows, knees, and hips.

7. Aztec warriors did not use guns. Their main weapons were spears, and clubs edged with razor-sharp pieces of volcanic glass known as obsidian (**G**). They also fashioned this into swords and knives.

8. It is unlikely that the Aztecs knew how to make panes of glass. Their doors and windows were covered with cloth to allow fresh air to circulate (**H**).

9. The Aztecs did not use fountain pens or ballpoint pens and they had no alphabet. Instead they wrote in pictures, known as glyphs (**I**). They did, however, make paper from the treated bark of wild fig trees.

10. Sneakers were not part of Aztec dress. They wore sandals consisting of a leather sole, supported at the heel with cloth and tied with a length of cord (**J**).

Funeral of a Viking chief

1. No electric streetlights existed in the Viking Age. Instead, burning torches (**A**) would have been used.

2. A typical Viking house would not have had a tiled roof. The rafters would have been covered with straw thatch or turf (**B**).

3. Although Hedeby was an important trading center, you would not have found a lion skin from Africa there. Historians believe the Vikings may have reached the shores of Africa, but they did not trade with the people there. The skins of bears (**C**), deer, wild boars, and even polar bears were traded for use as clothing and bedding.

4. The Vikings did not have radios for entertainment. Instead, poets composed long poems or *sagas* which told stirring tales about Viking gods and heroes. These were often recited at banquets (**D**).

5. Drinks would not have been served in glasses, but in beakers of wood or drinking horns (**E**).

6. Although the Vikings sailed far and wide across the seas, they did so without the aid of the compass. To navigate, they used a sunboard which worked in the same way as a sundial, and a sunstone (**F**). This was a crystal which changed color when held at a certain angle to the sun — even when it was overcast!

7. Warriors did not have cannons to defend their homelands. They relied on swords (**G**), spears, axes, and bows and arrows.

8. There were no lighthouses to signal to returning longboats. Burning torches (**H**) would have been placed on the headlands.

9. The Vikings did not sail in modern yachts but in wooden longships (**I**). Their bows and sterns were often carved in the shape of savage animals.

10. No crucifix would have been worn by a Viking since Christianity was not introduced until 832 A.D. The Vikings worshipped many gods (**J**) the most important being Odin. Our days of the week are named after Viking gods.

Mogul celebration

1. The Moguls did not have electric fans to keep the court cool. They relied on punkas, large fans made of palm leaves, or ceiling fans made of heavy rugs (**A**) which were operated by hand.

2. In Akbar's time you would not have seen a skyscraper like the Empire State Building (built in New York City in 1931). Instead, beautiful forts, mosques, and palaces (**B**) were built during his reign, including the famous fort at Agra.

3. Akbar's court would not have had stained glass windows. The Moguls did make glass, but used it to create bottles, bowls, and dishes, often covered with intricate decoration (**C**).

4/5. The Moguls played neither badminton nor cricket, but polo (**D**) has been played in the east for thousands of years. Akbar loved polo so much that he invented a rule allowing them to play in the dark, using a piece of burning wood instead of a ball.

6. The gramophone was not invented until the late 1800s. In Akbar's time the only music was provided by the court musicians (**E**).

7. The Moguls did not have cameras to record important events. Instead, they were captured in detailed paintings commissioned by the emperor (**F**). They often illustrated scenes from the daily life of the court or important historical events.

8. It would have been unlikely to see a court musician wearing a Turkish fez. He would have worn a turban (**G**) made by wrapping a length of silk around a small cap.

9. This court musician would not have been playing a Welsh harp. Instead, he would have played a traditional Indian instrument such as a sitar (**H**) which is played much like a guitar.

10. There was dancing in Akbar's court, but it would not have involved couples waltzing. The waltz is a ballroom dance that did not become popular until the 1800s. Instead, women would have performed traditional Indian dances to entertain the emperor and his visitors (**I**).

Minoan port

1. The Minoans were the first great sea power, but their ships did not look like this nineteenth-century clipper ship. Instead, Minoan boats had a single mast and a large, square sail (**A**). Some of their boats were nearly 100 feet long.

2. You would not have found the skull and crossbones, a pirate flag from the 1800s, flying from the mast of a Minoan galley. The Minoans did not have flags, but decorated their ships with traditional symbols (**B**).

3. This style of painting would not have existed in Minoan times. Paintings usually took the form of frescoes (**C**) decorating the walls of villas and palaces. This fresco shows athletes somersaulting over the horns of a charging bull. The bull was sacred to the Minoans.

4. Minoans did not have steel drums. Instead, they made huge pottery jars, called pithou (**D**) in which they stored olive oil, wine, and grain.

5. Neither did the Minoans have cardboard boxes. Instead, they made simple wooden crates (**E**).

6. The Minoans did not have forklift trucks to help them unload cargo. They would have carried the goods on their backs or in baskets (**F**).

7. Minoan palaces did not have crenellations or turrets. Instead, the symbol of the sacred bull's horns decorated the rooftops, and appeared over shrines and on pillars throughout the palace (**G**). One of the most important palaces was at Knossos, the Minoan capital of Crete.

8. This Minoan woman would have sewn her clothes by hand, making beautiful dresses with flounced skirts. She may, however, have used a loom to make the material (**H**).

9. The Minoans, like many ancient people, believed that the Earth was flat. They would not have had a world globe, but they did draw maps of the heavens (**I**) on clay tablets.

10. The Minoans were great craftsmen and fashioned many objects from gold, silver, copper, and bronze, but not telescopes. They used such precious metals to make beautiful jewelry (**J**).

The Emperor's visit

1. Begun in 214 B.C., China's Great Wall is the world's longest, stretching for 1,500 miles. The soldiers and peasants that built it did not have cranes to help them. They had only simple ladders and scaffolding of wood tied with ropes (**A**).

2. The ancient Chinese would not have had a modern wheelbarrow, but they did invent a more primitive version (**B**) in the second century A.D. It was called a wooden ox.

3. Han craftsmen made many beautiful objects such as this famous bronze "flying horse" (**C**). But they would never have made this model of the Eiffel Tower. The original was not built until 1889 in Paris, France.

4. The ancient Chinese would not have used money that looked like this. They minted their first coins in about 220 B.C. The coins were round with holes in the middle (**D**).

5. Chinese children would not have had toy cars to play with, but they had plenty of other toys and games, including hoops, kites, board games (**E**) and even toy soldiers.

6. The ancient Chinese were excellent carpenters. They did not have electric drills, but made use of a great variety of tools such as saws, hammers, axes, and chisels (**F**).

7. There were no hang gliders in ancient China, but silk kites of all shapes and sizes have been flown there for over 3,000 years (**G**).

8. You would not have found the dragon and Saint George, a legendary English knight, on a Chinese flag. In ancient China the dragon was a god and also a symbol of good luck. Its image appears everywhere — on imperial robes and flags (**H**) as well as part of festival costumes.

9. Wealthy women would have worn shoes with stacked, platform soles (**I**) rather than high heels.

10. There were no railways in ancient China. Goods were transported using a network of roads and canals. There were many wheeled vehicles, including carts, wagons, fancy carriages, and large boats that looked like modern sampans (**J**).

Return of the Inca army

1. Incas did not have camels. They used the closely related llama (**A**) to help transport goods through the mountains.

2. Inca soldiers would not have worn trousers, but woven tunics, cloaks, and elaborate leggings (**B**).

3. The Incas had not invented glasses, but they were advanced in other areas of medicine. They treated brain tumors by removing part of the skull, an operation known as trepanning. They also replaced teeth using silver crowns similar to those used by dentists today (**C**).

4. No Inca men grew beards. They were all clean shaven (**D**). When the Spaniards arrived, the Incas mistook them for the bearded saviors mentioned in their oracles. They welcomed them, believing that they had been sent by the gods.

5. You would not have found a carved elephant tusk from Africa among the Incas' riches. Instead, there would have been drinking vessels or figurines made of silver and gold (**E**).

6. The Incas did not build suspension bridges across mountain ravines. Instead, they made bridges of straw, hand-spun rope, and twigs (**F**).

7. The Incas had no horses or wheeled vehicles of any kind. They traveled everywhere on foot, using a system of paved roads that stretched throughout the empire. Instead of riding in a carriage, the Inca chief would have been carried by his men in the imperial litter (**G**).

8. The Incas did not read or write, so they would not have had newspapers. Many aspects of daily life were recorded on a *quipu* made of knotted lengths of string (**H**).

9. You would not have found a carving of the Madonna on an Inca temple wall. The Incas worshipped many different gods and goddesses (**I**). Their most important divinity was Viracocha, the Lord Creator.

10. The Incas did not know of the existence of the planets or solar system. They worshipped both the sun and the moon, but thought of them as gods (**J**).